THREE SURE-SHOT STRATEGIES TO

FUTURE-READY YOUR RUBBER BUSINESS

Overtake The Competition and Fasttrack Your Business to the Top

THREE SURE-SHOT STRATEGIES TO

FUTURE-READY YOUR RUBBER BUSINESS

Overtake The Competition and Fasttrack Your Business to the Top

VIDHI BHAGAT

Available on amazonkindle

Worldwide Published by

Pendown Press

PREMIUM BUSINESS PUBLISHER

PENDOWN PRESS LLP

An ISO 9001 & ISO 14001 Certified Co.,

Regd. Office: 3767A, Kanhaiya Nagar,

Tri Nagar, Delhi-110035

Ph.: 8130886000, 9650072927

E-mail: info@pendownpress.com

Branch Office: 1A/2A, 20, Hari Sadan, Ansari Road,

Daryaganj, New Delhi-110002

Ph.: 011-45794768

Website: PendownPress.com

Edition: 2025

Price: ₹ 399

ISBN: 978-93-6338-829-1

Layout and Cover Designed by Pendown Graphics Team

Printed and Bound in India by Thomson Press India Ltd.

DEDICATION

To my father, Late Shri Gopal Krishan Bhagat, my first mentor and forever inspiration, the gentlest soul and fiercest believer in equality I will ever know, and living proof that true strength dwells in the softest of hearts.

TABLE OF CONTENTS

ACKNOWLEDGEMENTS

First and foremost, I would like to thank **my parents**, who gave me abundant love and provided a nurturing environment that encouraged learning, which enabled me to grow into an independent and self-confident person.

During my growing-up years, I witnessed how dedicatedly my family contributed to this business, which has always been like a sibling to me. I'm also grateful to my **extended family**, who have always set high standards for hard work and goal achievement in front of me.

My father, late Sh Gopal Krishan Bhagat ji and his elder brother, Late Sh Suraj Prakash Bhagat ji, have been exemplary figures like *karamyogis* for me.

I also want to thank **all my teachers and mentors** who have guided me, without whose support I would not have reached where I am. A special thanks to **my mentor and friend, Akshar Yadav**, who has been a great support and the driving force behind the publication of this book.

I want to thank **my husband, Aayush Kharbanda**, and **my family**, who have always supported me in both my business and the writing of this book. I want to especially thank **my son, Viraaj,** whose playtime was certainly compromised despite my best efforts while I wrote this book and while I built my business and worked on myself and my dreams.

I also want to thank **my team**, who always support me and are ready to run and soar alongside me. I want to specially mention my mother, **Smt Neelam Bhagat, MD of Paul and Company,** who has been a constant source of strength and support all along while I take risks and do out-of-the-box things.

I would also like to thank the companies we represent- the management, the presidents, the teams, along with the forums we are part of and other industry colleagues and stalwarts.

This book was written after closely understanding a few of our top customers, who were kind enough to spare a significant amount of time to share their journey and experiences. Even though every interaction with anyone from this industry is a revelation in itself, **I would like to thank our customers whose contribution to this book has been immense:-**

- Sh Kanwaljit Singh ji, MD, Dolfin Rubber Ltd, Ludhiana
- Sh Vijay Maini, Hindustan Tyre, Ludhiana
- Sh Rahul Radhu, Radhu Tyre and Radhu Products (P) Ltd, Meerut and Rudrapur
- Sh Rakesh Mishra, MD, RPL Tyres, Guldhar
- Sh Rajeev Bhasin, Asian Tyre Factory, Jalandhar
- Sh VK Dhingra, MD, VK Tyre, Meerut
- Sh Harjit Singh and Sh Kamaljit Singh, Brightway Rubber Industry, Jalandhar
- Sh Rajesh Sharma, Purchase Head, Ralson (India)Limited, Ludhiana
- Sh A.K. Chandra, Purchase Head, Metro Tyres, Noida and Ludhiana

- Sh Venugopal, Purchase Head, MRL Tyres, Delhi, Noida and Gujarat
- Sh VK Ohri, Purchase Head, VK Tyre, Meerut
- Sh Hanuman Prasad Bhathara, Manager-Raw Material, Poddar Tyres Ltd, Ludhiana
- Mrs Elcee, Purchase Manager, Emtico Tyre/ Malhotra Rubber

Even though I could not interview some others, **I can't miss acknowledging other manufacturers like** Sh Sanjeev Pahwa ji from Ralson(India)Ltd, Arun Poddar Ji from Poddar Tyre, Ludhiana, Sh Pali ji and Sh Mandeep Singh from Speedways Rubber, Sh Arvinder Pal and Sh Jaspreet Singh from Speedways Tyre, Jalandhar, Sh Rajinder Thakur from ARB conveyors as they are an integral part of my and my family's work in this region.

This is not the end — merely the tip of the iceberg in terms of perspective received from customers. In fact, this book has given a sense of renewed purpose. I will surely take perspective from our other esteemed and established customers and keep writing future books to ensure that the industry and I continue evolving to offer nothing but the best to our customers.

Finally, I would like to express my **immense gratitude to my publisher, Dinesh Verma, CEO of Pendown Press and his team** for adding value to this project and making the editing and publishing process seamless.

PREFACE

YOUR CHANCE TO OVERTAKE AT THE TURN

Your business is like your baby or your younger sibling. You've nurtured it, sacrificed for it, and worked day and night to bring it to where it is today, only to see a competitor suddenly leap far ahead.

It stings. It hurts. It feels unfair.

But it's also a wake-up call; it shows one thing: the game is changing.

So, the real question is:

What can you do, as a small, medium, or even growing rubber manufacturer, to make sure *you* and your business are ready for the future?

Let me show you a picture—

Imagine yourself driving on a winding mountain road. You see a slow-moving truck ahead. You know you have to overtake, otherwise you will be stuck in slow motion forever, **and the only space you can do it is at the next sharp turn.**

Yes, it's risky.

Yes, the timing has to be perfect.

But if you miss that turn, you might be stuck behind for hours.

That's exactly where the **rubber industry** is today.

The rubber industry is at a sharp curve — a critical turning point.

Like driving in the hills — the only chance to overtake is on the bend. Right now, it is that bend.

If you take action now, if you innovate and modernize now, you will overtake.

If you **hesitate, someone else will grab that opportunity.**

And this time, t**he gap they create** might not be 10 steps or 10 years. It might **feel like 400 years.**

Because the world is changing that fast.

So don't wait. **The future won't wait for you.**

This is your moment — to future-proof your business, to leap ahead, and to ensure that five years from now, **you're the one being followed, not the one left behind.**

Act, and you leap ahead. Wait, and the gap could grow so wide it may take decades to catch up.

This is your moment to future-proof, upgrade, and lead — or be left behind.

The choice is yours!

In the pages of this book, I will show you how to Future-Ready/ Proof your business in 3 proven ways, easily, efficiently, and practically. This book is versatile in its value and will benefit a range of manufacturers, from very small ones to large-scale ones.

If you are ready to lead from the front, let's turn the page and change the outcome.

FIRST THINGS FIRST: PUTTING IT ALL INTO PERSPECTIVE

Before we delve deep into the topic, which I am sure has made you curious, allow me to take a few minutes and a couple of pages to introduce myself.

I am Vidhi Bhagat, a third-generation entrepreneur and an Industrial Chemical and Raw Material Supply specialist, serving as a growth partner for more than 3500 manufacturers across the country.

My journey in this industry started in 2013, when I joined my family business. We started in 1961, we cater to multiple industries, and the industry we started with was the Rubber Industry itself. Hence, it holds a special place in my heart.

Today, in 2025, it continues to be one of the top industries we work with. The contribution of this industry to India's economy, the way it functions, and the resilience it has shown have never ceased to amaze me.

Every day, I immerse myself in the world of chemicals and raw materials, exploring their intricacies and applications. A friendly disclaimer: Please don't assume that, being a female, I must be sitting pretty in my fancy office or something all day.

The truth, in fact, is far from it: I visit a lot of my customers, at their plants and the smell of rubber compounding in a plant is all too familiar and I always have special footwear ready for plant visit days, as I am well aware I will return with carbon black sooted shoes!

I live and breathe this industry daily. We supply rubber, rubber chemicals, pigments, waxes, fillers and resins, and other additives to manufacturers making rubber goods like tyres, tubes, conveyor and other belts, rubber parts, and hoses, among others. I see huge potential for this industry today and in the years to come.

Over the years, we've worked with various manufacturers and have introduced and supplied new and reliable industrial chemicals and raw materials. Since the time I joined the business, my attitude has always been to try, unlike some who are restricted and not open to new opportunities! I am glad my father and I took this up, and here we are today! From the inception stage to understanding customer needs and finally introducing these products into our company's portfolio, I have been intricately involved every step of the way. So much so that today I have enough knowledge to write a book on this matter!

To be truthful, for me, Paul and Company has always been like a sibling whom I have grown up with- my entire family, my father and my mother, my uncles, and we all have worked passionately to make it reach where it is today.

Even if someone wasn't directly involved, they have contributed behind the scenes by extending support in helping us realise our dreams. My father, after my grandfather's death in 1994, till he passed away in 2016, was a front runner in the Industrial Chemical and Raw Material Supply Industry. He was a stalwart who was known for his ethical business practices, fair play, and vast knowledge about the industry and his products.

His focus, Paul and Company, was founded with the noble intention of providing customers with authentic materials and offering a seamless solution for their industrial chemical and raw material needs.

For business owners and purchase managers, the task of procuring various chemicals and raw materials for manufacturing can be daunting. By choosing Paul and Company as their supplier, the idea was and continues to be that they can rest assured that they are receiving genuine products, allowing them to focus on their core operations without the stress of sourcing materials.

The company's commitment to quality and reliability ensures that customers can trust them to deliver on their promise of hassle-free procurement.

I've also seen many companies grow manifold, and at the same time, have seen many get lost in corridors of obsolescence. We have observed that while some have cracked the code, others keep wondering what to do or do the things they should have done long back, when water has already flown under the bridge, and it's too late, when even the whale of actions result in ant-sized results.

You must be wondering why I am sharing this gold mine of information, when many big-shots from the industry are paying lakhs and crores of money to consultants from the BIG Four and others.

After all, if you implement all that is mentioned here in this book, you can catapult yourself to the league of successful companies, which are some that you have aspired to.

So, Why the Book?

One, being in love with this industry, it breaks my heart to see so many companies ignoring the obvious and not reaching their full potential. The same industry where someone is growing 20% YOY basis while others have to shut operations, while belonging to the same industry!

Two, I am unable to reach everyone personally due to time constraints, so this book is dedicated to small, medium and nearly large manufacturers, to share 3 sure-shot ways to Future proof your Rubber Industry Business which I have observed in my 12 year career in the Rubber Industry, and my family who has dedicated their life to serving this industry.

I am sure that you will find immense practical value in this book, and it will steer you profitably on your future course.

CHAPTER 1

Why Future-Ready Your Business?

The biggest question on everyone's mind today is: What to do to keep up with today's rapidly changing world and not fall behind.

Aisa kya karen ki race of relevance mein humara business relevant rahe.

Did you know?

The World Economic Forum (WEF) claims that 10 years down the line, there will be job roles that not only don't exist but are unheard of today.

Soon, you will hear job roles like Chief Sustainability Officer and Cyber Security Specialist. These are not heads of some country, but people who will be employed in companies like yours and mine.

In fact, their report predicts that in the next 5 years (this is a 2023 report):

By 2027, 83 million jobs will be lost, while 69 million new jobs will be created, leading to a net loss of 14 million jobs, or 2% of the total workforce.

- Secretarial and clerical roles, including bank tellers and cashiers, will decline the fastest due to automation.
- Meanwhile, demand for AI specialists and cybersecurity experts will increase significantly.
- Job growth will primarily be driven by the localization of supply chains and the transition to a greener economy.

India is on the path to becoming the 3rd largest economy by 2027. We are where other nations were.

PWC's 28th Annual CEO Survey for FY 24-25 mentions:

- Many Indian CEOs are aggressively integrating or are set to integrate AI and GenAI into their company's business products and processes over the next three years, not by choice but by compulsion.
- 43% of India CEOs (as against 38% globally) consider product or service innovation, to a large/very large extent, to be the most common reinvention action over the last five years
- 38% of India CEOs (as against 32% globally) have targeted a new customer base
- Major concern over technological disruption: Technological disruption remains top of mind for India CEOs, followed by macroeconomic volatility and inflation, and low availability of skilled labour. Disruptive technology was also listed by Indian CEOs who believe their companies will be viable for 10 years or less as one of the top two factors influencing their companies' low economic viability.

Which means already major CEO's believe change is the only constant.

Also, A SIDBI report on the Indian MSME sector published as recently as May 2025 mentions:

- MSMEs also face challenges pertaining to access to newer markets amidst competition from larger companies. According to the survey, a majority of the MSMEs have been slow to adopt modern channels to reach customers.
- 18% of surveyed MSMEs face intense competition and struggle to expand into new markets. Around 70% of the survey respondents continue to use traditional modes of marketing, which hinders their scalability and ability to remain competitive. Effective utilisation of e-commerce and digital marketing can provide MSMEs with improved access to new markets and customers
- MSMEs play a key role in achieving climate action and sustainability goals in India. More than one-third of the respondents in the MSME sector have adopted some form of sustainable practices; 31% of the respondents in the primary survey have adopted Energy-efficient lighting and machinery, and 21% have adopted Renewable Energy Sources. At the same time, 33% of the respondents have opined that limited awareness is the key challenge in the adoption of sustainable practices

Then how can businesses stay future-ready or prepare for upcoming challenges in this rapidly changing world?

A quick Google, or now today, a ChatGPT result of "Top 10 companies of the world" will yield this result:

As of February 20, 2025, the top 10 companies in the world by market capitalization are:

1. **Apple Inc.**: Approximately $3.678 trillion.
2. **Nvidia Corporation**: Approximately $3.28 trillion.
3. **Microsoft Corporation**: Approximately $3.11 trillion.
4. **Alphabet Inc. (Google)**: Approximately $2.05 trillion.
5. **Amazon.com Inc.**: Approximately $1.97 trillion.
6. **Saudi Aramco**: Approximately $1.8 trillion.
7. **Meta Platforms Inc. (Facebook)**: Approximately $1.655 trillion.
8. **Tesla Inc.**: Approximately $1.274 trillion.
9. **Berkshire Hathaway Inc.**: Approximately $1.043 trillion.
10. **Taiwan Semiconductor Manufacturing Company (TSMC)**: Approximately $1.042 trillion.

The list is dominated by technology-driven companies, but Aramco is also among the top 10.

There must be a common thread among all of them.

- While the world grapples with recession, energy/power crisis, wars, and ocean freight, how are they able to consistently deliver?
- How is their balance sheet in green?
- While we struggle to provide salary increments, they continue hiring top talent and distributing dividends!

A close analysis reveals the answer—they address the needs of the customer.

You might say, 'I am doing the same!' However, the difference lies in the approach.

We create a product and then look for customers, while they identify issues and problems, develop solutions, and let customers find them.

Think about this: I was spending too much time on my screen. Apple introduced a built-in feature to monitor screen time. I was holding my screen too close, Apple now notifies me if my screen is too close. Android followed suit by offering an app for this.

Take Meta as an example: There was a growing trend of reels, so they introduced a feature where users could let Instagram/ Meta automatically create a reel based on a song to keep up with the trend and involve more people who find themselves less creative at making and editing reels!

Similarly, Tesla has integrated high-end features into its vehicles to cater to customers seeking sustainable alternatives. They continuously work on giving new features while making them affordable!

But how do they get to know about this?

They reach out to customers, stay connected, identify their pain points, and then go back to the drawing board. On the other hand, most of us create a product, perhaps because we've seen it succeed elsewhere and feel we can replicate that model, though we do this with good intention, this may not work out as well for us.

This may not necessarily be true, as all of us are a brand, and we have some brand elements due to which our customer is associated with us.

For instance, someone might replicate your product, but they can't copy your way of doing business—your culture, your people, or the entire customer experience. One might argue that they could hire your staff, but remember: the same flower may not thrive in a different environment. And you never know—what you once considered a *khota sikka* (underestimated asset) in your setup may work many times better elsewhere!

So, coming back to what the top companies in the world are doing, these are the strategies that not only helped them reach the top but also stay there:

- They focus on solving customer needs.
- Customers express their needs, and these companies take them seriously, creating solutions based on real problems.
- They identify a problem first and develop a product to solve it, rather than creating a product and then searching for customers.

Companies like Alibaba, Amazon, Kindle, Spotify, Airbnb, Zomato, co-working spaces, Ola, Uber, and Netflix are hugely successful because they solve real consumer needs. There was a demand, and they provided a solution.

Most recently, in Tier 1 cities, services like Blinkit and Swiggy have addressed the problem of 10-minute deliveries! Customers wanted groceries instantly, while Amazon Fresh and BigBasket were offering next-day deliveries in designated slots. Now, Zepto, Blinkit, and Swiggy are delivering groceries in metro cities within just 6 minutes—so fast that even elders in the house jokingly ask, *"Was he already waiting outside with the order?"*

Now, you might argue that most of these are business-to-consumer companies, except for co-working spaces.

However, I want to highlight how companies worldwide are becoming increasingly solution-centric.

- **Asian Paints** made its business model highly data-driven. They can now accurately predict which product will sell at a specific store within the next two hours and have structured their delivery system accordingly.
- They also launched a **Paint Academy** to provide training for painters, ensuring skill development and brand loyalty.
- **Closer to home, Dolfin Tyres** created a **Tyre Size Directory** detailing the sizes of tyres for all car models way back in 2012. Before such information was available on Google, this directory was a goldmine for dealers.
- **TruckSuvidha** introduced a digital platform connecting fleet owners and customers, streamlining logistics.
- Many **chemical manufacturers in India** have started offering **technical advisory services**, enhancing customer support. They spend lakhs on their labs, which not only help them improve their product, but also to help customers in improving parameters of their end products.
- **IndiaMART** revolutionized B2B commerce by bringing buyers and sellers together on a single online platform.

These examples show that businesses that prioritize solving real problems and addressing customer needs are the ones that succeed and sustain growth.

That, my friend, is exactly why you and your business need to be 'Future-Ready'!

So, the next logical question is, how do I make my business Future-Ready?

Well, that is why this book exists.

Here are 3 Sure-Shot strategies to build a Future-Ready business.

CHAPTER 2

How To Future-Ready Your Business?

Three Proven Ways to Move from Uncertainty to Unstoppable

As we have already discussed and understood, the world is changing fast. Markets are shifting, technology is evolving, and what worked yesterday might not even be relevant tomorrow. We're living in unpredictable times. Prices are fluctuating, customers are changing, and competition is getting tougher by the day. For businesses in the rubber industry, there's one truth that stands out: only those who adapt will grow.

You can't build tomorrow's business with yesterday's thinking.

For rubber industry manufacturers, this isn't just a trend; it's a turning point. **The businesses that adapt now will lead tomorrow. Those who wait might be left behind, wondering where things went wrong.**

That's why we focus on how to make your business future-ready, not someday, but starting now. This is not about theories. It's about clear, practical action. You'll discover three proven ways that successful rubber manufacturers are already using to stay ahead of the curve and create long-term growth.

This chapter lays the foundation for building a business that doesn't just survive change, but thrives in it. Whether you're a small, medium, or near-large player in the rubber space, this is your opportunity to prepare for the future, protect your growth, and even pull ahead of competitors.

Here's what you'll learn in the following chapters:

1. **Aligning Your Market & Product Strategy:**

   How to align your market and product strategy to create a strong, sustainable business foundation, where your product mix actually matches what your customers need. Making what sells, not just what you've always made. Aligning your product mix to actual customer demand can protect you from overstock, margin loss, and slow-moving inventory.

2. **Developing a Resilient Business Strategy:**

   Learn how to plan for uncertainty—so you're not left reacting to problems, but prepared for them, whether it's due to supply disruptions, global issues, or sudden market shifts. We'll look at how to set up systems that help you deal with market shocks, cash flow crunches, or sudden order shifts.

3. **Using the 4C Framework to Beat Competition:**

   When competition becomes price-focused, many businesses panic. But smart businesses use the 4C model—Capital, Customer, Communication, and Competition—to protect profits, build stronger customer relationships, and grow even in a price-sensitive market, by freeing up capital, leveling up customer service, improving communication, and keeping a sharp eye on your competitive landscape.

Future-Readying Is Not An Option

These aren't one-time tactics. They're long-term tools. In the next three chapters, we'll break down each of these strategies in detail, with real examples, clear frameworks, and ideas you can start applying in your factory, office, or dealer network right away.

Your future business won't build itself. But with the right mindset and approach, you can build a business that's profitable, adaptable, and built to last.

A business ready for the future is not built by chance—it's built by choice, strategy, and courage. And the next few pages will show you exactly how.

Let's begin.

CHAPTER 3

STEP-1 Aligning Your Market & Product Strategy

A. Choosing the Right Market

A market is where buying and selling take place, but how do we choose the right one for our business?

> **Warren Buffett wisely advised, *"Never put all your eggs in one basket."***
>
> Taking this to heart, we have diversified our businesses. There's a lot of power in diversification—it aims to increase profits and mitigate risk.
>
> **However, diversification without a clear goal may not always be beneficial.**

There are several types of diversification, which I will briefly touch upon. A lot of people get confused with the various types of diversification, as everyone is diversifying in whatever direction they want, so I've tried to explain it simply below:

1. **Concentric Diversification**

   This involves modifying an existing product to cater to a different customer preference while staying within the same industry.

   Examples:

   - **A samosa brand introducing a cheese-filled** samosa to attract new taste preferences.
   - **Domino's offering paneer tikka pizza** in India to cater to local flavors.

2. **Vertical Diversification**

   Vertical diversification means taking control of part of the supply chain, such as acquiring a supplier or distributor. This reduces reliance on external parties and cuts costs.

   Amazon exemplifies this strategy—it started with book sales but later developed its own distribution and delivery networks.

   There are **two types of vertical integration:**

   a. **Backward Integration**: Acquiring a supplier to control production.

   - **Example:** Amul, originally a dairy cooperative, has invested in its own dairy farms to ensure quality control over milk production.

   b. **Forward Integration**: Moving closer to consumers by selling directly.

   - **Example:** Hindustan Unilever expanded from manufacturing products to establishing **direct-to-consumer platforms**, enhancing customer engagement.

- Many cosmetic and skincare brands are shifting from relying on Amazon and other platforms to **direct-to-consumer (DTC) models** for better control over sales and customer experience.

The **goal of vertical diversification is to cut costs and reduce dependency** on external suppliers, thereby minimizing risks related to delays or price fluctuations. However, it also increases risk—if the market weakens, investments in production can become costly liabilities.

3. **Horizontal Diversification**

This strategy involves **launching an unrelated new product line** that caters to the same customer base. The objective is to meet different needs within the target market.

Examples:

- **Bata**, originally a footwear brand, diversified into accessories like **bags and belts**, appealing to its existing customer demographic.
- **ITC**, which **initially focused on tobacco, later expanded** into **biscuits (Sunfeast), instant noodles (Yippee), and personal care products.**

4. **Related or Defensive Diversification**

Companies adopt defensive diversification when they face a **saturated market, declining product demand, or shrinking profits**. Unlike proactive diversification, this is a **reactive strategy** aimed at safeguarding profits and maintaining market stability.

Example: A **print newspaper launching a digital news platform** in response to declining print readership.

5. **Unrelated or Offensive Diversification**

   Offensive diversification occurs when a business expands **to capture a larger market share and challenge competitors.**

   Unlike defensive diversification, **the company is already in a strong position** and proactively seeks to boost profits by drawing customers away from rivals.

   Example: Bajaj, originally an **automobile company**, entered the **financial services** sector through **Bajaj Finserv**, directly competing with established banks.

6. **Conglomerate Diversification**

   Conglomerate diversification happens when a company enters an **entirely new industry** with products **unrelated to its core business**, targeting a **new customer base**.

   Examples:

   - A **movie theater chain acquiring a car wash business**.
   - A **tech company expanding** into **home security**.

This strategy is **high-risk** and is usually pursued by **large corporations** with **strong financial backing**, such as **WarnerMedia and Disney**. While it provides **stability by spreading risk** across industries, it also **introduces complexity**, requiring new management skills and potentially creating internal competition. Decision-making can also become slower.

Some Indian examples include:

- **Reliance**, originally a **petrochemicals company**, now owns **Jio (telecom), Reliance Retail (supermarkets), and Viacom18 (entertainment).**

- **Tata Group**, which began in **steel**, now has businesses in **tea (Tata Tea), aviation (Vistara, Air India), and IT (TCS).**
- **Aditya Birla Group**, known for **textiles**, expanded into **telecom (Vodafone Idea) and financial services**.

I'm sure you have all seen some diversification examples, and we are all guilty of diversifying without a strategy in place.

Now, how to find out what the best market for you is?

The Answer lies here: Your data will tell you what your market is!

Now, one would say, where is this found? Does it even exist? Yes, it does exist. There is a market in the world, *jo humare liye bani hai, and hum uske liye bane hain.*

The Right market for us.

But **how to find it?**

Let's define this first of all, before we move forward.

What I am about to share now might be something that you already know, or it could be a stark diversion from what you felt it was.

So, the next logical question is,

"***Ke is Best market ke Charitrik Gunn (Best traits) kya hain?***

- Treats You with the Utmost Respect – Doesn't treat You as just another Vendor or Supplier.
- Matches your Mental Level, talks about Growth, and is not merely focused on Credit, Discounts, and Schemes.
- Makes Timely Payments.

It might seem that this is an ideal scenario, and this kind of market doesn't exist, especially if one is sitting in India and dealing with Indian *"Desi"* customers. But such a market does exist, and we need to work on it.

I am not saying stop working with customers and industries that don't have this in place, but to prioritize the right market.

Finding Your Right Market: Bringing It All Together

Now that we've explored the various types of diversification and the importance of aligning your product strategy with the right market, let's bring it down to action.

You don't need guesswork to find your ideal market: you need insight. And that insight already exists in your own data.

- **Start by bringing all your data together in one place.** This includes sales figures, customer feedback, payment history, and engagement patterns. Once consolidated, take a close look at your top-performing customers. Identify those who contribute the most revenue, offer the highest margins, or show the fastest growth.
- **Next, compare this customer set to the traits of the ideal market we discussed earlier:** respectful partnerships, growth-oriented mindsets, timely payments, and mutual value creation. You'll likely notice some patterns emerging—maybe they come from the same sector, belong to a specific industry, or show similar behavior and mindset.

- **These shared characteristics**—both demographic (like geography, industry, company size) and psychographic (attitudes, buying behaviour, values)—form the blueprint of your right market.
- **From here, build a template based on this ideal customer profile.** This becomes your filter, helping you prioritize and pursue markets where you are most likely to win—and where both you and the customer thrive in a long-term, win-win relationship.

In short, your right market isn't a mystery. It's hidden in plain sight—within your own data. All you have to do is observe, listen actively, and align smartly.

B. Focusing on the Right Product Category

Once **the right market is selected**, where we can be the best and continue to excel, we must shift our focus to the **right product or product category**.

Right now, **what product are we known for?** Is it something customers actively demand (*maang ke leke jaata hai*)? **Is it a push sale or a pull sale?**

- Did we create the product, or is it **demand-driven**?
- If we have a **Hero Product**, that's great—we should focus on **creating more Hero Products**.
- If we **don't** have a Hero Product, our priority should be to **develop one**.

We'll discuss **Hero Products later** in the following pages.

The Four Key Aspects of a Product Mix in the Tyre & Rubber Industry

A company in the **tyre and rubber** industry may offer a diverse range of products, and its product mix can be analysed using four key dimensions.

Here **I am using** the **example of a tyre manufacturer to help you understand how this works:**

1. **Width**: This refers to the number of different product lines a company offers.
   - **Example: Bridgestone**: Produces **tyres, industrial rubber products (hoses, belts), automotive components, and even sports equipment (golf balls, tennis balls).**
2. **Length**: This is the total number of products across all product lines.
   - **Example:** A **tyre manufacturer** with multiple product lines – and offers **5 types of car tyres, 8 truck tyres, and 4 industrial rubber sheets**, the product mix length is **17**.
3. **Depth**: This measures the variety within a particular product line, including different specifications, sizes, tread patterns, and performance features.
   - **Example:** A **truck tyre line** may include **all-season, off-road, and high-performance** options, each in multiple sizes.
4. **Consistency**: This refers to how closely related the product lines are in terms of function, production, and distribution.
   - **Example:** A company making only **tyres for different vehicles** has high consistency, while one producing **tyres,**

rubber gloves, and flooring has low consistency. A **well-planned product mix** helps a business **expand its customer base, increase sales, and strengthen its brand presence**.

These are some of the popularly used key terms often used when analysing a company's product mix. To make these concepts easier to understand and more relatable, practical examples from a tyre manufacturing company have been included above, illustrating how each dimension applies in a real-world context.

Your Company's Product Mix Should Include Three Types of Products:

Once during a meeting with one of my customers, I found him very upset, he felt that no matter what he made, the customer always demanded something else.

I don't have what they want, and what they want will take time to make, or at other times, they feel my capacity is already utilised, so what to do?

The answer is to have a product mix that covers your best sellers, upgraded versions of best sellers, and some rare/niche products.

In fact, you could even **keep some manufacturing capacity empty** to keep a buffer for some unexpected orders coming from customers. It might also help in getting those extra orders if your competitor's manufacturing book is full or they lack capacity. Or, in case you receive an opportunity to fulfill some out-of-the-box customization orders, you will not end up saying no; rather, you will be able to leverage that opportunity.

1. **Regular or Bestseller Products**: The **bread and butter** of the company, typically contributing **40-60% of total sales.**
2. **Upgraded Versions of Bestseller Products**: Enhancements to existing products that allow **upselling for higher profits.**
   - **Example:** A tyre with **better durability or enhanced grip.**
   - **Example:** A product tailored for **specific use cases or customer needs, say a conveyor belt that can withstand extreme conditions.**
3. **Rare or Niche Products**: Innovative, **R&D-driven products** that are **truly unique and not widely available in the market.**
   - **Example:** Companies working on **100% green tyres and some conveyor belts used in the food industry that require a completely different set of products.** They get better returns on their manufacturing!

It might take you some time to reach the right mix best suited for your product and your customers, some go via the hit and try method, while other manufacturers rely on their data. Data is the true kind in this age of information and technology.

Don't worry if you don't have data- monitor the production on a weekly, monthly, or quarterly basis to experiment and reach the right level.

Innovation & Technological Obsolescence is REAL

As far as your product mix is concerned, remember, technological obsolescence is a reality, and businesses must continuously **innovate to stay ahead.**

We've seen examples of companies failing to innovate at the right time.

For example, the Ambassador car and Nokia phones refused to innovate and adapt at the right time when it was important, and the world witnessed **their fall from such dominant shares to nothingness.**

Some companies take inspiration from other manufacturers, but to adapt them for your organization and your company, you need some technical prowess.

For example, when Chevrolet and Ford launched in India, they failed to adapt their models and pricing for the Indian Context, leading to a classic Copy-paste-fail situation.

- **Investing in R&D is crucial.** At least **one dedicated person** should be working on **research and technical advancements**. I'm not suggesting we increase costs, but we must adopt a mindset of innovation, because in today's world, staying relevant means constantly evolving.
- **A strong strategy team** is essential to guide product development and market positioning. This team could start with just one person, and that person could be you. Aapki company mein Strategy ka jhanda kisi ko lehrana padega. Agar aap aaj se 2-5 years ahead nahi soch rahe toh ho sakta hai aap game loose kar rahe hain.

By maintaining the right **product mix and innovation strategy**, businesses can ensure **long-term success and competitiveness**.

C. Zeroing in On A Hero Product

In marketing, a **hero product** is a standout item in a brand's lineup that captures the most attention, drives the highest sales, or strongly defines the brand's identity.

It's often the **best-selling or most popular product** and acts as a gateway for customers to explore the brand's other offerings.

Hero products embody the **brand's values, quality, or innovation** and are prominently featured in marketing campaigns to build recognition and loyalty.

A hero product –

- Attracts new customers,
- Generates buzz,
- And establishes a brand's reputation, making it a crucial part of the overall product strategy.

You Have Created a Brand – Now, What Are You Known For?

Your hero product is the reason customers come to you.

You can see Hero Products everywhere; every industry, every market has some hero products.

Examples of Hero Products Across Industries:

1. **Apple**: iPhone, then MacBook, it started the opposite, but today people enter the Apple universe with an iPhone

2 **Honda (Two-Wheelers)**: Activa, the name has become almost synonymous with the scooty

3. **Toyota**: Innova. Most innova owners exhibit a particular trait: they trade in their old innova for a new innova

4. **Ray-Ban**: Aviators & Wayfarers, their classic aviator style is what most people identify with, and it is quite copied

Hero Products in the Tyre & Rubber Industry:

1. **TVS Eurogrip**: **Durapro** (stronghold in two-wheeler segment)
2. **MRF**: **MRF ZVTS** (popular for passenger cars)
3. **Apollo Tyres**: **Apterra** (premium SUV & off-road tyre)
4. **BKT Tyres (Balkrishna Industries)**: Global leader in OTR, agricultural, and mining tyres
5. **Fenner India (JK Group)**: **V-belts & industrial hoses** (widely used in manufacturing & automotive industries)
6. **Trelleborg India**: **Rubber expansion joints & anti-vibration mounts** (used in industrial machinery & construction)
7. **Havells (Standard Rubber Cables)**: **Rubber-insulated electrical wires & cables**

The Key idea is to **identify, build, and promote** your hero product while expanding your other offerings.

The companies mentioned above, and many small and medium-sized ones, have also found their niche. Let's focus on how you can create a Hero product for your company and industry.

What Could Be Your Hero Product?

Would you like help identifying or refining your **hero product** based on your industry? I've created a 5-step guide to create your hero product and keep on creating on a regular basis. However, that would take another book in itself, though! If you are interested, do reach out to me at the details mentioned at the end of this book, and we will take it further.

Now here we move on and focus on the next crucial pillar in our future readying journey.

D. Innovating Continuously

Every day, competitors launch new products, and customers develop new preferences. Their demands are endless! We have two choices: **give up and say, "Enough, we can't do more," or rise to the challenge and continue delivering the best to our customers.**

Once, at a conference, I met a tyre manufacturer who was going through a similar dilemma and was on the verge of giving up. They had been in the business for over 20 years. I introduced myself as a distributor with a difference. Even though they weren't from my region, I shared insights on the importance of innovation and highlighted the costly failures companies have faced by ignoring it. He appreciated my perspective, found real value in our conversation, and eventually benefited greatly. Since then, he has referred us to many others in the industry.

To stay ahead of the curve, **constant innovation** is crucial. A company must not only compete with others but also challenge itself to keep improving. **Where can we innovate?**

Innovation is the key to staying ahead and delighting customers, making us their first choice. We see some examples of failures to innovate- like Blackberry- they had a great product, people went crazy about their BB pin, and with WhatsApp coming in, it made it open for all, and kaboom, they failed to innovate and adapt, and thought they would enjoy their cash cow situation forever.

Another example that you must have noticed is the Kodak reel- they failed to see the digital revolution, and even though they had seen huge success in reel cameras and reels, their failure to adapt at the right time proved costly for them. Perhaps they could have planned to diversify into making digital phones, which eventually replaced cameras. That would really have been strategizing and thinking 5-10 years into the future.

So, there are three broad areas where innovation is essential:

1. **Product Innovation**: Enhancing the product's performance, efficiency, durability, and load-bearing capacity.
2. **Customer-Centric Innovation**: Actively seeking feedback from customers and understanding their evolving needs. What the customer desires today will be a need tomorrow!
3. **R&D-Driven Innovation**: Investing in research and development to create new products and improve existing ones. This can also be done, keeping the future and competition in mind

There is continuous innovation and collaborative innovation, which we touch upon later. Types of innovation that can be undertaken under each of the above, and the goal can be:-

1. **Innovation to improve** the **end product**

   We need to keep seeking feedback from customers and investing in research and development to innovate for new products and improve existing products.

   Whether your customer is the end user or passing the product on to their own customers, their needs and feedback should directly shape your innovation and improvement efforts.

2. **Innovation to get more efficiency and output from raw materials**

   We need to constantly evolve the raw material going into the product, else one day we'll have an obsolete or expensive product, and no takers

3. **Innovation to create a pull strategy from the customer**

   Whether your customer is the **end user** or a **distributor who is part of the supply chain**, innovation should be tailored to meet their specific needs. This can also include how fast the material is reaching the customer.

   I want to share the example of JK Tyre, whose sales by the late 2000s were flagging, and they faced increasing competition from MRF, Apollo, and global brands like Bridgestone and Michelin. Rising raw material costs squeezed margins, and the demand for fuel-efficient, long-lasting tyres left JK Tyre lagging in technology.

They decided to focus on radial technology and sustainable materials.

They introduced India's first Smart Tyre with embedded sensors for real-time pressure, temperature, and wear monitoring and targeted fleet operators, offering predictive maintenance and cost savings.

They also developed low rolling resistance tyres using high-silica compounds, reducing fuel consumption.

- The result was that their sales increased by 15-20% following these innovations.
- They strengthened their B2B presence with OEM deals from Tata Motors, Ashok Leyland, and Mahindra.

There is another way to take up innovation, which is Collaborative innovation.

You can collaborate with Startups, universities, and suppliers who have R&D centres

- Indian companies can reduce dependency on foreign technologies by working with **startups** for localized solutions. Startups bring agility and new, unheard technologies.
- **Universities** offer testing facilities- when in business, one might not want to test this much. Universities foster a culture of trying again and again till you succeed. They help accelerate product development and commercialization. Universities help bridge the gap between theoretical research and industrial application.
- Indian companies can tap into Ph.D. research for product innovation
- Suppliers with **R&D centres** can co-develop indigenous alternatives to imported raw materials.

Examples from the Indian Context

Collaboration Partners	Focus Area	Innovation Outcome
Apollo Tyes & IIT Madras	Sustainable & Smart Tyre Technology	Low-rolling resistance tyres, bio-based rubber, AI-based sensors.
Nocil & Rubber Research Institute of India (RRII)	Advanced Rubber Chemicals	Eco-friendly rubber chemicals, high-performance additives, reduced carbon footprint.
Balkrishna Industries BKT & European R&D Institutes	Agricultural & OTR Tyres	Special tread compounds, radial tyre tech for farming, and automated tyre testing.
Fenner India (JK Fenner) & Industrial Machinery OEMs	Industrial Power Transmission	Customized V belts, water-resistant rubber compounds, and predictive maintenance solutions.
CEAT Tyres & Mumbai University (Nanotech Department)	Nano-enhanced Rubber Compounds	Silica-reinforced rubber, light-weight, heat-resistant materials & nano-additives for grip.
GRP Ltd. & Automotive OEMs	Reclaimed & Recycled Rubber	Integration of reclaimed rubber in auto parts & low-emission processing tech.

Phoenix Conveyor Belt India (Continental) & Cement/ Mining Companies	Energy-Efficient Conveyor Belts	Fire-resistant belts. real-time wear tracking, rubber-polymer composites.
TVS Srichakra & EV Startups	EV Specific Tyres	Low-resistance tyres, silent tyre tech, and self-healing compounds.
HASETRI & Global Universities	Advanced Elastomers Testing	Synthetic elastomers, improved rubber testing methods, and biodegradable rubber compounds.
Unipatch Rubber Ltd. & Retreading Industry	Tyre Retreading & Repair Materials	High-temperature resistant tyre patches, sustainable adhesives, and long-life retreading solutions.
Reliance Industries & IISc Bengaluru.	Carbon Capture & Green Hydrogen	Development of carbon capture technologies & green hydrogen solutions for clean energy transition.
TVS Motor Company, IIT Madras & Suppliers.	Locally Designed, Electric Scooters.	Developed India's first indigenous e-scooter, TVS iQube, reducing dependency on Chinese components.

E. Leveraging Sustainability

Sustainability means using the Earth's resources in a way that meets our needs today *without* harming the ability of future generations to meet theirs.

We see serious problems around us:

- Rising temperatures due to climate change
- Animals are going extinct
- Forests are being cleared
- Hills are being broken for hotels, and constant mining.

All of this is damaging our environment and disturbing the balance of nature.

In a country like India, though, getting people to act on such issues isn't always easy. We saw this during the COVID pandemic; many didn't take precautions like wearing masks until the government stepped in with strict rules or penalties.

The truth is, in many cases, people only adopt new behaviours when there's either a strong push (a *danda*) or a clear incentive. And that's why, when it comes to sustainability, we need to make the benefits obvious, the steps simple, and the message loud, because protecting the planet isn't just a government job. It's everyone's responsibility.

Yet some Indian early adopters didn't wait for government policies to launch environmentally friendly initiatives, and they gained significantly in their business: for example, Reva, the EV, which has now been taken over by Mahindra Electric.

India's **first electric car, REVA, was introduced in 2001,** long before government incentives for EVs were in place. It sort of pioneered the EV movement in India, eventually leading to its acquisition by Mahindra, which is now a key player in the electric mobility space.

This is just one of the examples among many, and each of the businesses took a proactive approach toward sustainability, proving that waiting for policy changes isn't always necessary for success, and they made it big.

Today, the idea is to earn from sustainability, and Indian companies are stepping up their sustainability game in a big way. Nearly 90% of the country's top corporations have solid sustainability strategies in place, and about half of them are aiming for net-zero emissions. Businesses are also realizing that going green isn't just good for the planet, it's good for profits too.

Some Initiatives in the Tyre Sector:

- **Sustainability-Linked Financing:** JK Tyre & Industries secured a $100 million Sustainability-Linked Loan from the International Finance Corporation in January 2025. This funding is designated for expanding energy-efficient tyre production at their plants in Madhya Pradesh and Uttarakhand, aligning with India's green initiatives.
- **Recycling Initiatives:** Epsilon Carbon has invested in a tyre recycling facility in Karnataka, aiming to process 30,000 tonnes of tyres annually. This facility will produce 9,500 tonnes of recovered carbon black and 12,000 tonnes of tyre-

derived oil, contributing to a circular economy in the tyre industry.

Overall, while Indian companies are making big strides in sustainability, there's still a long way to go to ensure these efforts are deeply integrated into business operations.

Two common terms used when sustainability is mentioned are green manufacturing and circular economy.

Green manufacturing is a comprehensive approach aimed at reducing the environmental impact of production processes while enhancing efficiency and sustainability. This concept integrates various practices designed to minimize waste, conserve energy, and utilize eco-friendly materials.

When I share what the Circular Economy is, you might smile. This is what at least people born in or before the 80s have experienced.

A **circular economy** is an economic system designed to **eliminate waste, reuse resources, and create a sustainable production and consumption cycle**. Unlike the traditional **linear economy**, which follows a **"take-make-dispose"** model, a circular economy aims to **keep materials, products, and resources in use for as long as possible** through recycling, refurbishing, and regenerating natural systems.

We can go on and on about this concept, but perhaps we'll leave it for some other time.

For Indian businesses, going green is no longer just a moral choice—it's a strategic move for higher profitability, market expansion, and long-term resilience.

Those who embrace sustainability today are setting themselves up for a competitive edge in the future. Some examples of these are as below: -

1. **Cost Savings Through Energy Efficiency**

   Indian businesses are increasingly turning to energy efficiency as a smart way to cut costs. For example, Tata Motors has reduced its operational expenses by adopting solar and wind power solutions across its plants. According to the Bureau of Energy Efficiency (BEE), companies that invest in energy-efficient equipment can save between 20% and 30% on electricity bills. While residential electricity rates are being kept low due to election-driven promises, commercial and industrial units are facing rising power costs, making energy efficiency even more critical for long-term savings.

2. **Increased Consumer Demand for Sustainable Products**

   A 2023 Nielsen report found that **73% of Indian consumers** prefer brands that are environmentally responsible. And brands like Patanjali and Tata Consumer Products have seen a surge in demand for their eco-friendly, chemical-free goods.

3. **Government Incentives and Tax Benefits**

   The Indian government is actively encouraging businesses to go green by offering a range of financial incentives. One such initiative is the Perform, Achieve, and Trade (PAT) scheme, which rewards companies for reducing their energy consumption. Additionally, businesses investing in renewable energy can claim tax benefits under Section 80-IA of the Income Tax Act. For example, a company earning INR 10 crores annually from an eligible solar power project could save approximately INR 3 crores per year in taxes—assuming a 30% corporate tax rate—amounting to around INR 30 crores over a decade.

4. **Access to Green Financing and Investments**

   The Reserve Bank of India (RBI) has included green projects under **Priority Sector Lending (PSL)**, making it easier for businesses to secure loans. PSL is an RBI mandate requiring banks to allocate a specific portion of their lending to sectors deemed vital for economic development, including agriculture, micro, small, and medium enterprises (MSMEs), and renewable energy. By classifying green projects under PSL, the RBI ensures that these sectors receive the necessary financial support to thrive.

Key Provisions for Green Projects

Loan Limits: Bank loans up to ₹30 crore for purposes such as solar-based power generators, biomass-based power generators, windmills, micro-hydel plants, and renewable energy-based public utilities (e.g., street lighting systems, remote village electrification) qualify under PSL. pib.gov.in

- **Individuals:** Loans up to ₹10 lakh per borrower for renewable energy projects are also included under PSL.

Benefits for Businesses: Easier Access to Credit:

- **Incentivized Lending:** Banks are motivated to meet PSL targets, making them more inclined to finance green projects.

- **Simplified Approval:** The PSL classification often streamlines the loan approval process for eligible green projects.

Indian conglomerates like Reliance and Adani are attracting billions in green funding. Reliance Industries raised **$4 billion** in green bonds to expand its renewable energy business.

5. **Compliance with Global Trade Standards**

   The EU's **Carbon Border Adjustment Mechanism (CBAM)** is pushing Indian exporters to adopt low-carbon practices or face trade barriers. If they don't comply, they'll be out of business. How Arvind has implemented Zero Liquid Discharge(ZLD):

   - **Arvind Envisol:** Arvind Ltd. established a dedicated subsidiary, Arvind Envisol, specializing in developing and implementing ZLD solutions for the textile industry.
   - **Technology adoption:** Arvind utilizes advanced wastewater treatment technologies like Multi-Effect Evaporators (MEE) to achieve near-zero liquid discharge.

6. **Brand Loyalty and Reputation Boost**

   - Companies with strong ESG (Environmental, Social, and Governance) performance have outperformed the market by **3% annually** over the last five years (Morningstar India).
   - ITC's "Well-being Out of Waste" (WOW) initiative enhances its brand image while improving waste management.

Why Sustainability is Important for India

India has unique challenges that make sustainability a bigger priority compared to developed nations:

1. **Rapid Industrialization and Urbanization:** India is growing fast, but this growth comes with high pollution levels, waste management issues, and resource depletion. Sustainability is essential to balance progress with environmental responsibility.
2. **Severe Pollution and Climate Risks:** Indian cities rank among the most polluted in the world. The country also faces rising sea levels, extreme heat waves, and water shortages, making sustainability urgent for long-term survival.
3. **Energy Dependency:** While India is pushing for renewable energy, it still heavily relies on coal and oil. Transitioning to solar, wind, and hydrogen-based energy is crucial for energy security and sustainability.
4. **Regulatory Push:** The Indian government has introduced stricter ESG norms, mandating corporate sustainability disclosures. Industries that fail to adapt risk losing business and facing legal consequences.
5. **Economic and Social Impact:** Sustainability in India isn't just about the environment—it's also about job creation, rural development, and inclusive growth. Green initiatives, such as electric mobility, renewable energy, and sustainable agriculture, create employment opportunities and drive innovation.
6. **Global Competitiveness:** As global markets move towards sustainable sourcing and carbon-neutral supply chains, Indian businesses must align with these trends to remain competitive internationally, especially if one is exporting to a country focusing heavily on sustainability measures.

Why so much stress on Sustainability measures, though?

Sustainability is no longer optional—it's essential for survival. Globally, companies are adapting to climate risks, resource constraints, and changing consumer preferences. In India, the stakes are even higher due to pollution, urbanization, and regulatory shifts. Businesses that embrace sustainability now will not only protect the environment but also future-proof themselves against economic and regulatory risks. Else, what are we leaving behind for future generations? A solid foundation to build upon or a generation who'll be busy cleaning and reversing the mess this generation has made.

Building a Greener, Stronger Tomorrow

The question is no longer "Should we embrace sustainability?": The question is "How fast can we make it central to everything we do?"

Sustainability isn't just about tree-planting drives or CSR checkboxes. It's a business imperative, a growth driver, and a responsibility we carry,not just toward the planet, but toward our people, our profits, and our future.

Whether it's through energy-efficient operations, green financing, tapping into the growing consumer demand for responsible brands, or aligning with global trade norms, every step towards sustainability is a step toward long-term resilience and leadership.

Indian businesses now stand at a crucial crossroads.

- One path leads to short-term thinking, cost-cutting, and reactive compliance.

- The other leads to strategic investments in sustainability, innovation, and value creation—not just for shareholders, but for society at large.
- We must shift our thinking from "compliance" to "competitive edge," from "what's the minimum required" to "what's the maximum possible." Those who act early and decisively will not only reduce their environmental footprint but also expand their market share, deepen customer loyalty, attract premium funding, and build brands that endure.
- The time to act is now. Not when the rules force us. Not when the damage becomes irreversible. But now, because those who lead on sustainability will lead the market.

Let's be among them.

CHAPTER 4

STEP-2 FROM CHAOS TO CONTROL:

MANAGING UNCERTAINTIES THROUGH STRONG SUPPLIER PARTNERSHIPS

In today's time, the only certain thing is: Uncertainty *Hogi hi Hogi*- the only thing certain in today's rapidly changing world is uncertainty!

In this section, we touch upon why we need to counter market uncertainties and also the type of strategies to counter these. First, we need to understand the types of uncertainties that can occur

1. **Demand-related uncertainty**
2. **Supply-related uncertainty**

Demand, as in demand for your end product, uncertainty might be there. Are we manufacturing first and then looking for customers? The previous section of this book covered this part. Now, this section of the book is more focused on supply-related uncertainty.

Why do uncertainties happen, though?

They happen due to both internal and external factors. Many times, external factors are truly external, and one cannot do anything about them. There is zero control over situations like wars and pandemics!

However, internal factors are internal to us and our organisation, and these are where we should focus. We can create an internal system or strategy to counter external situations and be prepared to handle them well.

External Factors include:

- **Market:** what happens in the market, demand dies, and demand grows. When we ask the customer, then demand *nahi hai*, and suddenly they'll call a few days later, *material dedo*(give)!

  For example, one never thought the introduction of UPI would lead to a decrease in toffee sales at ITC! Lots of *Kiryana* stores would give toffees instead of loose change while returning the money. Since UPI came in, people were even paying 35 paise or 10 paise as their bill rounded up, and no toffee transactions are needed anymore!
- **Geopolitical Matters:** we all have seen that the Ukraine-Russia war has disrupted supplies of various products, including Butyl rubber, raw material for precipitated silica, among others. There was a situation when I received a call from a frantic customer, who was not importing rubber, about what would happen to local Rubber prices when Israel shot the first missile at Iran. Even if you are not depending on

imported materials, we are all connected to global supplies of a certain product. One of the 4 resorcinol manufacturers in the world- the one based out of the USA closed its unit overnight; the world had 25% less resorcinol overnight!

- **Natural Disasters and Pandemics:** We all have seen the pandemic firsthand and experienced the challenges that came with it. During this period, due to the small shelf life of latex, and due to high demands-units were asked to open!

Various types of internal risks can be incurred **at any organization**:

- **Operational Risks**: equipment failure, *supply chain disruption*
- **Safety Risks**: accidents, fire, hazardous material leaks
- **Financial Risks**: raw material price fluctuations, delayed payments
- **Compliance Risks**: not meeting environmental or labour regulations
- **Cybersecurity Risks**: system hacks, data loss

You may also use past incident reports, audit data, and employee inputs to build this list specific to your organization and industry.

Even though some situations are out of our control, we need to keep working towards decreasing the same, and the only way to counter this is strategic planning, and having short-term, medium-term, and long-term strategies to counter this. We'll also touch upon top tips to keep in mind to ensure minimum supply chain uncertainties.

***Here are* 5 ways to plan and prepare for supply chain disruptions**

A. Risk Management: Plug the Gaps Before They Drain You

➢ **Risk Assessment**

We must be fully aware of risks and gaps in our supply chain, otherwise we might focus on the wrong areas of improvement, and as a result, we would be in the same place where we were..

Identify Risks: Conduct a comprehensive assessment to identify potential risks and vulnerabilities in the supply chain. This can be done by identifying what material frequently keeps going out of stock or the reason why the factory is not giving the desired output.

➢ **Risk Prioritization**

Simply make a list of all materials and star-mark the ones that are causing issues. We should focus on these first and the rest later. You never know what surprises businesses throw up! Prioritize risks based on their likelihood and potential impact on the supply chain-

- Likelihood: Low / Medium / High
- Impact: Minor / Moderate / Severe

If you find 2-3 things or items that are causing issues, then identify the major breakdown that is happening due to which product. The higher risk item/issue will cause more loss as compared to others. We need to focus on all, but priority and focusing on the severe and moderate-impact issues first is important

➢ **Risk Mitigation**

Develop and implement risk mitigation plans for high-priority risks. A plan can be as simple as I will look for more suppliers for this product, or I will look for what product can replace this product.

For each high-priority risk, answer:

- Can it be prevented? If yes, how?
- If not, how can we reduce its impact?
- What's the backup plan if it occurs anyway?

B. From Transactions to Trust: Future-Proofing Through Supplier Partnerships

Supplier Relationship

Just like one needs a like-minded customer, one also needs a like-minded vendor/ partner/supplier to ensure you reach the top. Here's how you can go about it.

➢ **Strong Relationships:** Build strong relationships with key suppliers to ensure cooperation during disruptions. Communication is the key to building a strong relationship. All relationships need care and nurturing! After all, we are human beings! I have collated a list of Tips to build strong relationships.

➢ **See Them as Partners, Not Just Vendors**

Bring them into the loop early, whether it's new product ideas or long-term plans. When both sides work together, everyone grows.

- **Recognise Good Work**

  A simple thank-you or a quick note of appreciation can really strengthen your relationship. Don't forget to acknowledge milestones or long-term collaborations, too.

  - **Keep Communication Clear and Consistent:** Share what's coming—forecasts, timelines, and any changes. Being transparent helps avoid surprises and builds trust.
  - **Pay on Time (or Early):** Settling invoices on time—or even early at times—goes a long way in building credibility. It also shows you value their role in your supply chain. Payment discipline and compliance are the need of the hour. When we look at nations ahead of us in the top Economy race, this might be the detrimental factor.
  - **Be Upfront About Problems:** If something's off-track, let them know early. Most suppliers try to support you if you're honest and proactive.
  - **Understand Their Side of the Business:** Take the time to learn about how they work—their capacity, challenges, or peak seasons. It helps you make more realistic requests and builds mutual respect.
  - **Negotiate with a Long-Term Lens:** Push for value, not just the lowest price. Fair negotiations show you're in it for the long haul, not just the next deal.
  - **Stick with Them in Tough Times:** If they're going through delays or disruptions, a little flexibility from your end can earn serious loyalty. Support in tough times is never forgotten. If you treat them like an option, one might reciprocate the same! Vice versa is true too!

Collaborative Planning with Suppliers

Engage in collaborative planning with suppliers and logistics partners to ensure alignment and quick responses to changes. In the small and medium industry segment, **I have seen** that **customers are** wary **of demand forecasting.**

The ***Typical answer is pata hi nahi.*** This is a standard copied answer across the industry! *Pata hi nahi* is taking the company somewhere else only.

If you want to go from Delhi to Chandigarh, will it work if you have no milestones, no Google Maps? How much more time will it take, and you didn't take a wrong turn? That just won't work.

This reminds me of the hindi song- ***"Jana tha Japan pahuch gaye Cheen Samajh gaye na!" And pyaar ka to pata nahi but stress zarur ho jayega!***

There must be tight coordination of production, work, sales, and store planning.

When the biggest companies on earth with massive scales of operation are able to do it, then why can't we do it?

We must rise up to the challenge, get mental buy-in from our team, and see that things are done. If not 100%, at least 60% would be done. It's better than being 100% in the dark.

If you know and don't want to share, as unsure due to rates and actual demand, mention that this is an estimation.

Strategic Partnerships

We've already discussed how this helps in the previous point, in the case of your vendor. There are two other areas I would like to touch upon

- **Industry Collaboration:** Collaborate with industry peers to share resources and information during disruptions. Good relations and collaborations go a long way. We have some customers who were not very organized but would give some material on loan to each other if a lorry got late. Today, with ERP and GST implemented, people are wary of giving material on loans, but sometimes I've seen even the top companies, their plants have come to a standstill due to rigid policies.

  I am sure they have good reasons based on bad past experience, but one needs to have a slightly realistic and flexible approach to life and business, especially when we are living in times of huge uncertainty. I know it might sound like an inadequacy of your team, but at the same time, I must reiterate- great teams make great organizations! The Team might need empowerment, or maybe it is an actual issue. I don't recommend that this be made a routine affair, though, but agile(flexible or in Hindi *"Furtila")* business is the need of the hour.

- **Logistics Partnerships:** Form multiple strategic partnerships with reliable logistics providers to ensure flexibility and reliability.

Supplier Diversification

What if the situation is truly out of hand for then your supplier might or might not be able to support it. The second approach to keep in mind is to **source materials from multiple suppliers across different regions to reduce dependency on any single supplier.**

- Having a s**ingle supplier for critical products might be counterproductive** if their systems break down or there is some issue at the customer's end.

- **For non-critical products**, identify one alternate supplier and give them maybe just a 5% share of orders.
- **For critical products,** one Indian and one imported supplier must be identified, and see what market share mix works best for your organization.

C. Smart Tools, Smarter Business: Make Technology Your Best Friend

Some people are scared of technology; they feel it is too fast-paced. Even though I have felt so at times when it comes to social media, my nieces and nephews use some apps that I take some time to understand, as they are different from what I have used earlier. However, not understanding them immediately doesn't disrupt my life. If those Apps are still around later, I can always figure them out eventually, like many of our elders got the hang of Facebook and Instagram gradually.

However, **when it comes to technology use in our business, one might lose out in the race if technology is not adopted at the right time.**

I know people who are using AI to invest like Warren Buffett, to write code like Bill Gates, and to create marketing and sales strategy for their business like a marketing biggie like David Ogilvy or Philip Kotler would! I even recently came across a video where a manufacturing unit used AI for quality checks!

Predictive Analysis

We are in such times that data is the power. IT giants are talking about big data, your phone is listening to what you are saying and then showing you an ad, we as simpletons can at least use predictive analytics to forecast potential disruptions and demand fluctuations.

Latest Alerts: If some material is of huge interest, one can subscribe to updates regarding that product to stay abreast of what is happening around the world with respect to this product. To set up Google Alerts, start by visiting google.com/alerts in your web browser. In the search bar labeled "Create an alert about...", enter the keywords or phrases you want to monitor. Google will then display sample alerts to help you assess the relevance of your chosen terms. To fine-tune your alerts, click on "Show options" or the gear icon to access advanced settings. Here, you can customize how often you receive alerts (such as instantly, daily, or weekly), select the language and region of the content, and filter sources like news sites, blogs, or websites. You can also decide how many results to get per alert and choose your preferred delivery method, such as receiving them via email.

Real-time Monitoring

Implement real-time monitoring systems to track supply chain activities and identify issues early.

- A robust mechanism of how material is stocked and stored, and what the low supply levels are- can help in this
- Many manufacturers already use this kind of rolling stock list to ensure no stockouts happen

Inventory management and Demand forecasting

This part of technology today is a very crucial component; we'll discuss this in detail in the next point.

D. Stock Smart, Sleep Easy: The New Rules of Inventory Management

Safety Stock

Maintain safety stock levels to buffer against supply chain interruptions. Ensure buffer stocks are not played with, regardless of how easily the material is available. Be like the mother who ensures that if her child wakes up hungry in the middle of the night, she is well stocked on atta, potatoes, and milk to feed the child!

Demand Forecasting

- Software/ System Being used for Inventory management: Use advanced demand forecasting techniques to optimize inventory levels and reduce stockouts or overstocking.
- Develop in-house systems or hire software developers to help with demand forecasting and to ensure sufficient material is in stock. Your forecast must include stock in transit- this gets missed at times, as software shows only the inventory on hand.
- We at Paul and Company follow an inventory management system developed by Eli Goldratt, and it is mostly helpful unless some material's critical shortage happens worldwide. This factors in seasons, uses a rolling average of 3 months, and includes buffer stock, lead time, and how much time it will take from order to delivery, not just dispatch!

Are You Using The Best-Suited Software/System for Inventory Management?

Is your software up to date? Is it using AI, is it integrating things like auto email or auto WhatsApp, or is it primitive like Tally? I have nothing against Tally, Indian Chartered Accountants love Tally. Though Tally is now offering apps that share reports. The big 4 love SAP, yet to finalize books, they use Tally. Whatever you use, it needs to give a timely business update, and it should not be used just to finalize the balance sheet. Reports are a must in today's time to make fast decisions.

Lack of Clearly Defined Reorder Triggers

Are you that business where no clear minimum/maximum levels or reorder points are set for each item? If yes, review and reset. Otherwise, you run the risk of emergency orders, production stoppages, and higher freight costs for urgent sourcing.

E. When the Unexpected Strikes: Be the Business That's Ready with a Backup Plan

- **Flexible Manufacturing:** Implement flexible manufacturing processes that can quickly adapt to changes in supply and demand. For example, materials should already be tested beforehand, which are replacements; sources should already be identified, and materials of different makes should already be tested.
- **Adjustable Production:** Use modular production techniques to easily adjust production volumes and product mixes. This basically means that you can semi-prepare some products

beforehand. This also means you need to have a mix of big and small machines. In case some chemical is less but sufficient for a smaller batch, this should not deter you from making a smaller batch of product.

- **Robust Supply Chain:** Design supply chain networks with resilience in mind, considering alternative routes and backup suppliers. Resilience means it can withstand changes.
- **Financial Preparedness:** Maintain strong financial health to absorb the impact of disruptions. Financial liquidity is the king in such times, and one can really earn money. During the pandemic, countries were disposing of their materials in the sea! And some manufacturers made a hay day out of this, due to strategic buying, they eventually paid off debt and raised enough money to set up new plants! Solvent and synthetic rubber prices hit rock bottom. Sometimes, some deals also come up, like for high seas sales that work on upfront payment only, hence this is needed.
- **Insurance:** Obtain comprehensive insurance to cover potential losses from supply chain disruptions.

Here are some situations where businesses that thought the insurance was a waste were covered, and the insurance expenses paid off.

Another example, a small tech firm thought cyber insurance was overhyped and was planning to skip it. A data breach led to stolen customer data, legal issues, and compensation claims. Cyber insurance covered fines, legal costs, and PR efforts to restore their reputation. You might have heard about WazirX- the platform that deals in cryptocurrency. They had a security breach, due to which they lost a lot of customer money, and due to a lack of insurance, everyone is suffering, and it has become one of the most disregarded platforms in the country!

The most famous example:

Wimbledon had **pandemic insurance** as part of its event cancellation policy, purchased annually since the **SARS outbreak in 2003**. When **COVID-19 forced its cancellation in 2020**, the **insurance paid out around £114 million ($142 million USD)**, covering losses from tickets, broadcasting, and sponsorships. Over 17 years, they paid **£30 million in premiums**, making it a highly successful risk management decision. This highlights how insurance can seem unnecessary—until it becomes a financial lifesaver.

Don't wait for a crisis to make your risk mitigation strategy. It's much easier to build backup options when the business is stable than under pressure.

Tips to Build Resilience in Uncertain Times

➢ **Proactively Map Supply Chain Risks**

- Create a "vulnerability map" for your supply chain, categorizing materials and processes based on their likelihood of disruption and impact severity.
- Regularly update this map, especially during global events or economic shifts.

➢ **Create a Supplier Diversification Scorecard**

Don't depend on just one vendor for critical vendors. Use a scorecard that ranks suppliers based on pricing stability, delivery timelines, backup support, and response in crisis. This helps in faster decision-making when disruptions hit. Some top tyre manufacturers give month-on-month vendor ratings.

- **Turn Tech from a Cost into a Catalyst**
  - Invest in predictive tools that monitor raw material trends and automate reorder alerts.
  - Use software that not only tracks inventory but also integrates real-time updates across departments.
- **Run "What-If" Business Simulations**

  Conduct quarterly or half-yearly drills with your team: What if a raw material doubles in price? What if a port shuts down? Treat them like fire drills, so when the fire comes, you're calm and prepared.

  - **Build a "Supply-Crisis Handling Document"**

Document clear SOPs (Standard Operating Procedures) for supply shocks: whom to call, what steps to take, fallback suppliers, alternative materials, communication templates, etc. This keeps your team aligned during chaos.

CHAPTER 5

COUNTERING COMPETITION WITH THE 4C FRAMEWORK

Now we come to the last section of the book.

In the first section, we discussed customers and the market. The second part was about the supply chain. This section is dedicated to countering competition effectively.

We all often feel like competition is our biggest enemy. I want to give a new perspective on this, if you don't already possess the same. If there were no competition, none of us would be working on giving a better experience to our customers.

Life is not just a flat line; there are ups and downs. Without competition, we would just resonate at the same level and never focus on improving ourselves. Even though our main competition is against ourselves only, external competition keeps us on our toes. It helps us avoid becoming complacent.

Some industries or their customers have suffered due to a lack of competition.

Like in telecommunication industry in India-though in many countries, a few companies control the telecom sector and to ensure this doesn't happen in India - the Indian Govt has ensured Vodafone doesn't crash, but even though we still enjoy lowest data charges in the world- they have increased; recently due to a lot of mergers and acquisitions in the Airline Industry we have seen rises in airfare in the past couple of years;

In the early years, Microsoft had no competition. When Mac OS and Linux came in, they were encouraged to improve themselves

Some downsides of not having healthy competition are:

- **Higher Prices:** Consumers pay more due to a lack of alternatives.
- **Lower Quality:** No pressure to improve services or products.
- **Slower Innovation:** Companies don't need to improve if there's no competition.
- **Market Manipulation:** Large firms can dictate terms and suppress smaller players.

I have developed the 4C Framework to counter competition in a healthy and productive manner and recommend using it to not just survive, but thrive. I am sharing it with you below in detail, so you can implement it easily and effectively.

1. **Competitive Analysis**

   Even though competition is against ourselves, to excel in what we do and be better from one day to the next, we need to be well aware of what the competition is up to., t.

   This is because you never know when your competition could silently creep in and take over your business. Also, sometimes competition doesn't look like competition - we have already discussed the Toffee Killer example for ITC. Another example is Netflix. Who do you think is the biggest competition for Netflix? Prime? Jio Hotstar?

   No.

Think again- it is sleep.

Once I realised this, even though I kept my subscription after degrading to a basic plan, I decided to sleep and focus on myself, my family, and my work. Some reasons why competition should be closely followed: -Keeping track of competitors is essential for businesses to stay competitive, innovate, and adapt to market changes.

Here's why it matters, with real-world examples:

1. **Market Trends & Innovation:** Observing competitors helps businesses stay ahead and quickly adapt to new technologies and trends.

   Example: Apple and Samsung monitor each other's smartphone innovations. When Samsung introduced foldable phones, Apple had to consider future adaptations. In fact, when Apple launches new features that render some apps useless in their app store, at the same time, they thrive in the Android store, or developers are pushed to include these new features.

2. **Pricing Strategies:** Understanding competitor pricing ensures effective product positioning, whether through competitive pricing or differentiation.

   Example: Budget airlines like IndiGo and SpiceJet frequently adjust fares based on competitor pricing to attract customers.

3. **Customer Expectations:** Competitor actions shape customer expectations, pushing businesses to enhance services and features.

   Example: In the automobile sector, if one brand offers free servicing for five years, others may follow to retain customers.

The pricing has to be done as per that and cater to the new normal.

4. **Marketing & Branding Strategies:** Tracking competitor marketing strategies helps businesses refine their advertising approach.

   Example: Coca-Cola and Pepsi continuously tweak their advertising based on each other's campaigns, launching counter-strategies to maintain consumer interest.

5. **Identifying Market Gaps & Opportunities:** Competitor analysis highlights gaps in the market, leading to new opportunities.

   Example: Patanjali's entry into the herbal FMCG market prompted Dabur and HUL to expand their herbal product lines. They never realised the demand for this segment, and here the competitor did it for them, and they were forced to wake up and act

6. **Benchmarking & Performance Analysis:** Comparing performance with competitors allows businesses to measure their success and improve.

   Example: Walmart constantly evaluates competitors' pricing and operations to stay ahead in the retail sector.

7. **Strategic Planning & Innovation:** Learning from competitors' successes and failures informs strategic decision-making.

   Example: Netflix closely watches competitors like Disney+Hotstar and Amazon Prime Video to adjust its content and pricing strategy. What content is a hit or a miss gives an idea of where to focus next.

8. **Customer Retention & Loyalty:** Competitor analysis helps businesses develop better loyalty programs and retention strategies.

   Example: If a competitor launches a successful loyalty program, other companies must improve theirs to retain customers. This is seen a lot in action in the hospitality sector or service-related industries.

9. **Supply Chain & Cost Efficiency:** Observing how competitors source raw materials and negotiate with vendors can improve cost efficiency.

   Example: In the manufacturing industry, if a competitor secures better bulk pricing for raw materials, Paul and Company might explore similar negotiations.

10. **Regulatory & Compliance Awareness:** Keeping an eye on competitors' responses to regulatory changes helps businesses stay compliant and prepared.

    Example: When India introduced BS-VI pollution norms, automakers like Maruti Suzuki and Tata Motors quickly updated their engines. When Maruti decided not to focus on Diesel engines, others stepped up to cover the Market share Maruti was giving up.

11. **Risk Management & Business Survival:** Awareness of competitors' responses to challenges helps businesses mitigate risks.

    Example: During COVID-19, restaurants observed competitors shifting to online delivery and quickly adapted to survive. Zomato and Swiggy helped the restaurants in shifting, so much so that even hotels started new wings for deliveries.

Hence, we see that *competition pe nazar rakhna bahut important hai.*

2. **Capital (Free It Up)**

   I am sure all of us have faced situations of stuck capital or working capital issues from time to time. We can create a system to get out of this. I am sure you would agree that capital is the blood of our business. Blood not flowing properly is not good for the body, and the absence of proper cash flow is counterproductive for the business. Here are some ways that capital can be freed up - it could be stuck in raw materials, finished goods, or with customer/compliance

   I. **An inventory management system should be followed for raw materials.** Lower inventory levels might lead to stockouts, which lead to loss, and also the issue faced is of procuring this material at a higher cost than normal, or paying more freight if the quantity is less. Another issue is too much inventory. Recently, one of the customers discovered they were ordering material, whereas some new labour/stock in charge was not stocking materials properly, and they discovered they already had 2 months' worth of material in the store. The worst part of it was that some material had already expired!

   II. **Check if the Finished goods inventory is very high. Be aware of the inventory levels,** some strategy - even a one-page strategy to follow when stocks go out of control should be followed to ensure capital is not stuck.

   You can give it a name like the overflow strategy. Prepare a list of prospective customers for that product. Offer them a deal.

You can even offer an incentive to your staff, over and above the special incentive already being given.

You might argue with me that the material is stuck, it is expensive, and I am suggesting that you pay more incentive than normal, decreasing profits even more.

Yes, I agree, but trust me, the losses coming from the material that will get stuck for a longer duration and the cost of carrying that inventory will be much higher. Ultimately, the customer wants fresh material, so the more you delay, the more you lose profit while increasing inventory carrying costs.

Such an opportunity should also be used to recognise the employees who are ensuring that the stuck stock moves.

*However, be alert that the same person is not delaying the sale by overstocking to get the recognition & reward!

III. Capital Stuck in Compliance/ Customer

One needs to act fast when capital gets stuck here, and legal action is unavoidable. Many advisors and consultants support in this regard.

3. Customer Service

I. Today, the customer is using various new platforms and services and is used to an amazing level of service, instantly.

II. They are accustomed to very different levels of service. Platforms like Zomato even track and tell you where your order is at the moment.

III. Today's customer is dictating the terms now.

IV. Today, bad service might cause a brand image to take a hit, and things to spiral out of control instantly. Recently, I went to a newly opened Starbucks - their washroom was not clean, their service was poor, it's not that I was judging, but when one calls themselves the best in the business, they have a lot to live up to their name and promise.

Examples of next-level service experiences are numerous:

Amazon is giving updates, Zomato and Swiggy are giving no-questions-asked refunds.

When **Indigo Airlines** faced a viral complaint about rude staff behaviour, it had to respond quickly to control the damage. In India, where social media amplifies issues, brands must maintain strong customer service to avoid PR crises. This is not just relevant when a crisis happens; your service game should be top-level all the time.

Do you know one of the FMCG Giants, Hindustan Unilever Limited, has a robust helpline number, and the CEO himself has one of the KRA points to take up the call himself and understand what are the issues being faced.

In today's time, we have to go an extra mile to delight the customer as they are spoilt for choice. How can you do this for your customers? It could be as simple as hiring a person or allocating responsibility from the current staff regarding grievance redressal.

4. **Communication**

Everything we discussed in Sections 1, 2, and 3 of the book ultimately comes down to one thing—our customers.

Interestingly, Japan compiles a list of "useless inventions" every year, and years ago, the selfie stick made that list! At the time, it seemed unnecessary, but it turned out to be an innovation ahead of its time.

This example highlights how important it is to stay aligned with customer needs—without that connection, even great ideas may not succeed, and we could be too early or too late for the party. Here, the party is the success of our own business, and being part of our customers' success. The best way to build a connection with your customers is through communication.

Key Takeaways on Customer Communication:

- **Maintain close communication with customers.** Strong and consistent communication builds trust, ensures smooth transactions, and helps address any concerns they may have. Whether it's about order updates, technical support, or simply strengthening the relationship, staying in touch is crucial for long-term success.
- **Be proactive and responsive.** Timely responses, personalized interactions, and proactive engagement make customers feel valued and appreciated.
- **Leverage digital communication when needed.** If in-person meetings aren't feasible due to distance, time constraints, or other reasons, make full use of digital tools. Phone calls, emails, video meetings, WhatsApp messages,

and other online platforms help maintain seamless interaction. Embracing these channels ensures continuity in business communication and keeps operations running smoothly.

Some examples of Indian Companies putting this to use:

The Titan Turnaround

Titan, India's leading watch brand, noticed that customers were looking for more than just traditional designs. There was a time it faced competition from imported brands like **Swatch**, or bigger brands like Casio, Esprit, Guess, and Tommy Hilfiger, and more notably, the iWatch and other smart watches.

- Through direct **customer surveys, store feedback, and online reviews,** they identified new trends. As a result, they **introduced** the **Titan Edge** - the world's slimmest watch based on demand for lightweight, sleek designs.
- They also **launched Titan Raga** – a collection of premium watches designed specifically for Indian women. **All** these imported watches and the smart watch don't go well with Indian ethnic wear, and a new opportunity was created.
- They also expanded into **smartwatches (Titan Smart, Fastrack Reflex)** to cater to tech-savvy customers.

The Mahindra Miracle

Mahindra, a leading Indian automobile manufacturer, has improved its SUV line-up significantly based on customer feedback. They conducted extensive surveys and discussions before launching the XUV700, which included:

- **ADAS (Advanced Driver Assistance Systems)**
- **Bigger infotainment system**
- **More powerful engine & better mileage**

The Result?

XUV700 became an instant hit, with bookings crossing **100,000 units in just 4 months!**

You might say I am sharing all examples of companies that are big, but now I'm sharing the example of BOAT. It was not a Tata or Mahindra from the start.

The BoAt Bonanza

BoAt, India's most popular homegrown audio brand, dominated the market by **listening to young Indian consumers.** Early feedback showed a demand for **affordable yet stylish wireless earphones.** Users wanted **sweat-resistant sports earphones →**

- Led to the launch of the **BoAt Rockerz series** for gym-goers. Gamers wanted **low-latency audio →** BoAt launched **gaming earbuds** with ultra-low latency.

Result: BoAt became the **No.1 brand in India's audio segment** by staying in tune with customer expectations.

By staying closely connected with customers—whether in person or digitally—we create stronger relationships, improve collaboration, and drive better results. This can also be a combination of what the competition is doing, but ultimately, the old adage comes to mind- ***Janta Janardan hai!*** They decide what they buy.

The Power of the 4C Framework

The 4C Framework—Competitive Analysis, Capital, Communication, and Customer Service is your compass in a fast-changing business landscape. It offers a sharp, actionable lens for strengthening your business.

- Staying aware of what your competitors are doing (**Competitive Analysis**) helps you anticipate moves and avoid complacency.
- Freeing up blocked or underused **Capital** gives you the financial muscle to reinvest in growth.
- Clear, consistent **Communication**—internally and with stakeholders—keeps everyone aligned and focused.

And finally, responsive, reliable Customer Service doesn't just retain clients, it builds your brand reputation from the ground up. When used together, these four pillars create a strong foundation for businesses to not just survive, but lead.

CHAPTER 6

THE FINAL WORD: FUTURE-READY, STARTING TODAY

To wrap up everything we've covered in this book –

We've taken a deep dive into **three proven strategies** that can help you **future-proof your business**. These are not just ideas; they are practical steps you can start implementing today to ensure your company is not only prepared for what's coming but thrives in it.

Whether it's strengthening your systems, embracing smart technology, building resilience in your supply chain, or being more in your customer's company, each step brings you closer to a more secure, scalable, and successful future.

Remember, the future doesn't arrive all at once.
You build it—one smart decision at a time.

1. **The first step** is to make your company **future-ready** by focusing on the **right market** and the **right product mix**. We discussed how to identify the right product to focus on and the **Hero Product** that can make you a winner! Along with this, one must also emphasize **continuous improvement, innovation, and sustainability**. In the **sustainability** segment, we covered the **circular economy** and **green manufacturing**, which we will delve deeper into in the near future.

2. **The second step and focus area** is adopting a **strategic approach** to counter market uncertainties. To achieve this, we first need to **analyze risks, manage them effectively, optimize supplier relationships, leverage technology, focus on inventory management, and have a solid backup plan** in place to ensure we are never caught off guard.
3. **The third and final step** covered the **4Cs to Kill Competition**, which are **competitive** analysis, freeing up **capital, customer** service, and **communication!**

I have put my heart and soul into this book, drawing insights from my family, who have dedicated their lives to serving this industry, and from my own experiences.

These insights are shaped by my interactions with various members of the rubber industry, our customers, the companies we represent, and other stalwarts in the field.

Due to the limitations imposed by **page constraints**, I regret that I could not elaborate further on certain concepts. As I conclude this book, I strongly feel that another book is needed to fully capture the enormity of this topic and some of the topics I have covered! While I have made every effort to convey **comprehensive** information within the allotted space, some topics could benefit from deeper discussion. In this fast-changing world, **ideas must be exchanged at the right time and put into action immediately**, but only after careful deliberation to ensure maximum returns on the actions taken.

I have sincerely **shared my knowledge through these pages**, but I would also like to urge the readers to feel free to connect with me at any time. My goal is to **help this industry thrive,**

grow, and stay relevant in changing times. I am actively working on all the areas mentioned in the book and might have additional real-world insights to share, especially regarding **sections 2 and 3**, which are particularly relevant to me, and I am actively applying them in my own business. Furthermore, I have personally assisted many manufacturers with the topics covered in **section 1**.

Additionally, I am developing a **framework to help you identify potential product issues in your production process**, and I will be sharing it soon.

Some concepts are best understood through **direct interaction**, whether through **in-person conversations, phone discussions, or interactive Q&A sessions**. These formats allow for real-time **clarification, deeper exploration**, and the opportunity to discuss **specific pain points** in detail.

Despite the constraints, I am sure this book has **added value** to its readers and provided **meaningful insights** or **key takeaways** that resonate with them. Every reader may extract a **unique lesson** or **perspective**, ultimately contributing to their **personal and professional growth**.

The journey doesn't end here…

turn the page and let's connect.

I invite you to a special Q&A session with me, Vidhi Bhagat.

Simply **drop a "Hi" at**

or **fill out the form** to connect!

I'm directly reachable at -

9711133719

Vidhibhagat@PaulandCompany.co.in

Www.PaulandCompany.co.in

Www.PaulandCompany.in

Notes

Notes

Notes

Notes